DISCARD

D1126999

AN AMERICAN PRIMER

AN
AMERICAN PRIMER
BY WALT WHITMAN

WITH FACSIMILES OF
THE ORIGINAL MANUSCRIPT

EDITED BY
HORACE TRAUBEL

AFTERWORD BY
GAY WILSON ALLEN

SCIRE QVOD
SCIENDVM

HOLY COW! PRESS • 1987

HOUSTON PUBLIC LIBRARY

R0158495411
HUM

COPYRIGHT, 1904, BY
HORACE TRAUBEL

Holy Cow! Press, 1987

ISBN 0-930100-24-7 (cloth)
ISBN 0-930100-23-9 (paper)

Holy Cow! Press
5435 Old Highway 18
Stevens Point, Wisconsin 54481

FOREWORD

The American Primer is a challenge rather than a finished fight. We find Whitman on this occasion rather laying his plans than undertaking to perfect them. It would be unfair to take such a mass of more or less disjointed notes and pass them under severe review. Whitman never intended them for publication. He should not be criticised, as he has been by certain American editors, for an act for which he is in no way responsible. The Primer is not a dogma. It is an inter-rogation. Even as a dogma something might be said for it. As a question it intimates its own answer. One of Whitman's remarks about it was this: " It does not suggest the invention but describes the growth of an American English enjoying a distinct iden-tity." Whitman would every now and then get on his financial uppers. Then he would say: " I guess I will be driven to the lecture field in spite of myself." The Primer was one of his projected lecture themes. The lecture idea had possessed him most convinc-ingly in the period that antedated our personal acquaintance. Leaves of Grass *appeared*

*before I was born. When I got really into
contact with Whitman the fight was on in
full fury. " The Leaves has always meant
fight to the world. It never meant fight to
me." That was what Whitman said of it.
He would make a point of my youth. " You
bring young blood to the field. We are
veterans — we welcome you."*

*Whitman at different times, especially in
the beginning, when he struck up his rebel
note, planned for all sorts of literary ven-
tures which were not consummated. Whitman was undoubtedly convinced that he had
a mission. This conviction never assumed
fanatic forms. Whitman was the most
catholic man who ever thought he had a mission. But he did regard himself as such a
depository. Yet he never believed or con-
tended that he possessed exclusive powers or
an extraordinary divination. He felt that
if the message with which he was entrusted
did not get out through him it would get out
through some other. But in his earlier career,
after he tired of writing in the formal way
and to the formal effect — for he played the
usual juvenile part in literary mimicry — he
felt that it would be difficult, if not impossible,
to secure publishers either for his detail work*

*or for his books. He often asked himself:
How am I to deliver my goods? He once
decided that he would lecture. And he told
me that when the idea of The American
Primer originally came to him it was for a
lecture. Yet these notes in themselves were
only fragments. He never looked upon them
as furnishing more than a start. " They
might make the material for a good talk," he
said. " It's only a sketch-piece anyway," he
said again: " a few rough touches here and
there, not rounding up the theme — rather
showing what may be made of it. I often
think the Leaves themselves are much the
same sort of thing: a passage way to something rather than a thing in itself concluded:
not the best that might be done but the best it
is necessary to do for the present, to break
the ground."*

*Whitman wrote at this Primer in the early
fifties. And there is evidence that he made
brief additions to it from time to time in the
ten years that followed. The most of the
manuscript notes are scribbled on sheets of
various tints improvised from the paper
covers used on the unbound copies of the
1855 edition. There is later paper and later
handwriting. But the notes were largely*

written in the rather exciting five years before the war. " That stretch of time after 1855 until 1861 was crowded with personal as well as political preparations for war." But after he had issued the first edition of Leaves of Grass, *and after he found the book surviving into the 1856 and 1860 editions, some of his old plans, this lecture scheme among them, were abandoned. The Primer was thenceforth, as a distinct project, held in abeyance. I remember that in the late eighties he said to me: " I may yet bring the Primer out." And when I laughed incredulously he added: " Well, I guess you are right to laugh: I suppose I never shall. And the best of the Primer stuff has no doubt leaked into my other work." It is indeed true that Whitman gave expression to the substance of the Primer in one way or another. Even some of its sentences are utilized here and there in his prose and verse volumes.*

In referring to the Primer upon another occasion, Whitman said: " This subject of language interests me — interests me: I never quite get it out of my mind. I sometimes think the Leaves *is only a language experiment — that it is an attempt to give the spirit, the body, the man, new words, new potentiali-*

FOREWORD

ties of speech — an American, a cosmopolitan (the best of America is the best cosmopolitanism) range of self-expression. The new world, the new times, the new peoples, the new vista, need a tongue according — yes, what is more, will have such a tongue — will not be satisfied until it is evolved." But the study brought to bear upon the subject in the manuscript now under view was never resumed. The Primer, therefore, is, as a part of Whitman's serious literary product, of marked significance. Whitman said of it: "It was first intended for a lecture: then when I gave up the idea of lecturing it was intended for a book: now, as it stands, it is neither a lecture nor a book."

As an alternate to his adopted headline I find this among Whitman's memoranda: "The Primer of Words: For American Young Men and Women, For Literati, Orators, Teachers, Musicians, Judges, Presidents, &c."

I have followed the original manuscript without any departures whatever. All its peculiarities of capitalization and punctuation are allowed to remain untouched.

HORACE TRAUBEL.

SOME FACSIMILES OF THE
ORIGINAL MANUSCRIPT

The Primer Of Words

For American

For American Young Men and Women,
For Literati,
Orators, Teachers,
Musicians,
Judges, Presidents,
&c

                                        fitness —
What is the ~~strange Charm~~
~~our~~ - What the ~~fitness~~ strange
Charm of aboriginal
names.⸺ Monongahela
(rep) - it rolls with
venison richness upon
the palate

A perfect user of words
uses things — they they exude
~~A po~~ in power and beauty
from him — miracles from
his hands — miracles from
his mouth — ~~the M~~ lilies, clouds, sunshine, woman ~~appeared expressing it~~, ~~things~~ whirled
like chain = shot — rocks,
defiance, compulsion,
houses, iron, locomotives,
~~—~~ the oak, the pine, the keen eye,
the hairy breast, the
Texan ranger, the
Boston truckman, the
~~the~~ woman that arouses
a man, the man that
arouses a woman...—

AN
AMERICAN PRIMER

MUCH is said of what is spiritual, and of spirituality, in this, that, or the other — in objects, expressions. — For me, I see no object, no expression, no animal, no tree, no art, no book, but I see, from morning to night, and from night to morning, the spiritual. — Bodies are all spiritual. — All words are spiritual — nothing is more spiritual than words. — Whence are they? along how many thousands and tens of thousands of years have they come? those eluding, fluid, beautiful, fleshless, realities, Mother, Father, Water, Earth, Me, This, Soul, Tongue, House, Fire.

A great observation will detect sameness through all languages, however old, however new, however polished, however rude. — As humanity is one under its amazing diversities, language is one under its. — The flippant read on some long past age, wonder at its dead costumes[customs?], its amusements, &c.; but the master understands well the old, ever-new, ever-common grounds, below

1

those annual growths. — The master, I say, between any two ages, any two languages and two humanities, however wide apart in time and space, marks well not the superficial shades of difference, but the mass-shades of a joint nature.

In a little while, in the United States, the English language, enriched with contributions from all languages, old and new, will be spoken by a hundred millions of people: — perhaps a hundred thousand words ("seventy or eighty thousand words" — Noah Webster, of the English language).

The Americans are going to be the most fluent and melodious voiced people in the world — and the most perfect users of words. — Words follow character — nativity, independence, individuality.

I see that the time is nigh when the etiquette of saloons is to be discharged from that great thing, the renovated English speech in America. — The occasions of the English speech in America are immense, profound — stretch over ten thousand vast cities, over millions of miles of meadows, farms, mountains, men, through thousands of years — the occasions of saloons are for a coterie, a bon soir or two, — involve waiters standing

2

behind chairs, silent, obedient, with backs
that can bend and must often bend.

What beauty there is in words! What a
lurking curious charm in the sound of some
words! Then voices! Five or six times in
a lifetime, (perhaps not so often,) you have
heard from men and women such voices, as
they spoke the most common word! — What
can it be that from those few men and
women made so much out of the most common word! Geography, shipping, steam,
the mint, the electric telegraph, railroads,
and so forth, have many strong and beautiful words. Mines — iron works — the sugar
plantations of Louisiana — the cotton crop
and the rice crop — Illinois wheat — Ohio
corn and pork — Maine lumber —all these
sprout in hundreds and hundreds of words,
all tangible and clean-lived, all having tex-
ture and beauty.

To all thoughts of your or any one's mind
— to all yearnings, passions, love, hate, ennui,
madness, desperation of men for women, and
of women for men, — to all charging and
surcharging — that head which poises itself
on your neck and is electric in the body
beneath your head, or runs with the blood
through your veins — or in those curious in-

3

credible miracles you call eyesight and hearing — to all these, and the like of these, have been made words. — Such are the words that are never new and never old.

What a history is folded, folded inward and inward again, in the single word I.

The words of *the Body!* The words of Parentage! The words of Husband and Wife. The words of Offspring! The word Mother! The word Father!

The *words of Behaviour* are quite numerous. — They follow the law; they are courteous, grave, have polish, have a sound of presence, and abash all furniture and shallowness out of their sight.

The words of maternity are all the words that were ever spoken by the mouth of man, the child of woman — but they are reborn words, and the mouth of the full-sized mother, daughter, wife, amie, does not offend by using any one of them.

Medicine has hundreds of useful and characteristic words — new means of cure — new schools of doctors — the wonderful anatomy of the body — the names of a thousand diseases — surgeon's terms — hydropathy — all that relates to the great organs of the body. — The medical art is

4

always grand — nothing affords a nobler scope for superior men and women. — It, of course, will never cease to be near to man, and add new terms.

Law, (Medicine) Religion, the Army, the personnel of the Army and Navy, the Arts, stand on their old stock of words, without increase. — In the law, is to be noticed a growing impatience with formulas, and with diffuseness, and, venerable slang. The personnel of the Army and the Navy exists in America, apart from the throbbing life of America — an exile in the land, foreign to the instincts and tastes of the people, and, of course, soon in due time to give place to something native, something warmed with throbs of our own life.

These States are rapidly supplying themselves with new words, called for by new occasions, new facts, new politics, new combinations. — Far plentier additions will be needed, and, of course, will be supplied.

(Because it is a truth that) the words continually used among the people are, in numberless cases, not the words used in writing, or recorded in the dictionaries by authority. — There are just as many words in daily use, not inscribed in the dictionary, and seldom or never in any print. — Also, the forms of grammar are never persistently obeyed, and cannot be.

The Real Dictionary will give all words that exist in use, the bad words as well as any. — The Real Grammar will be that which declares itself a nucleus of the spirit of the laws, with liberty to all to carry out the spirit of the laws, even by violating them, if necessary. — The English Language is grandly lawless like the race who use it — or, rather, breaks out of the little laws to enter truly the higher ones. It is so instinct with that which underlies laws, and the purports of laws, it refuses all petty interruptions in its way.

Books themselves have their peculiar words — namely, those that are never used in living speech in the real world, but only used in the world of books. — Nobody ever actually talks as books and plays talk.

The Morning has its words, and the Evening has its words. — How much there is in the word Light ! — How vast, surrounding, falling, sleepy, noiseless, is the word Night ! — It hugs with unfelt yet living arms.

Character makes words. — The English stock, full enough of faults, but averse to all folderol, equable, instinctively just, latent with pride and melancholy, ready with brawned arms, with free speech, with the knife-blade for tyrants and the reached hand for slaves, — have put all these in words. — We have them in America, — they are the body of the whole of the past. — We are to justify our inheritance — we are to pass it on to those who are to come after us, a thousand years hence, as we have grown out of the English of a thousand years ago : American geography, — the plenteousness and variety of the great nations of the Union — the thousands of settlements — the seacoast — the Canadian north — the Mexican south — California and Oregon — the inland seas — the mountains — Arizona — the prairies — the immense rivers.

Many of the slang words among fighting men, gamblers, thieves, prostitutes, are powerful words. These words ought to be collected — the bad words as well as the good. — Many of these bad words are fine.

Music has many good words, now technical, but of such rich and juicy character that they ought to be taken for common use in writing and speaking.

7

New forms of science, newer freer characters, may have something in them to need new words. — One beauty of words is exactitude. — To me each word out of the —— that now compose the English language, has its own meaning, and does not stand for any thing but itself — and there are no two words the same any more than there are two persons the same.

Much of America is shown in its newspaper names, and in the names of its steamboats, ships — names of characteristic amusements and games.

What do you think words are? Do you think words are positive and original things in themselves? — No: Words are not original and arbitrary in themselves. — Words are a result — they are the progeny of what has been or is in vogue. — If iron architecture comes in vogue, as it seems to be coming, words are wanted to stand for all about iron architecture, for the work it causes, for the different branches of work and of the workman—those blocks of buildings, seven stories high, with light strong façades, and girders that will not crumble a mite in a thousand years.

Also words to describe all American pecu-

liarities, — the splendid and rugged characters that are forming among these states, or
are already formed — in the cities, the firemen
of Mannahatta and the target excursionist
and Bowery boy — the Boston truckman —
the Philadelphian. —

In America an immense number of new
words are needed, to embody the new political facts, the compact of the Declaration
of Independence, and of the Constitution —
the union of the States — the new States —
the Congress — the modes of election — the
stump speech — the ways of electioneering
— addressing the people — stating all that is
to be said in modes that fit the life and experience of the Indianian, the Michiganian,
the Vermonter, the men of Maine — also
words to answer the modern, rapidly spread-
ing, faith, of the vital equality of women with
men, and that they are to be placed on an
exact plane, politically, socially, and in business, with men.   Words are wanted to sup-
ply the copious trains of facts, and flanges
of facts, feelings, arguments, and adjectival
facts, growing out of all new knowledges.
Phrenology.

Drinking brandy, gin, beer, is generally
fatal to the perfection of the voice; — mean-

ness of mind the same;—gluttony in eating,
of course the same; a thinned habit of
body, or a rank habit of body — masturba-
tion, inordinate going with women, rot the
voice. Yet no man can have a great voca-
tion who has no experience with women and
no woman who has no experience with men.
The final fiber and charm of the voice fol-
lows the chaste drench of love.

The great Italian singers are above all
others in the world from causes quite the
same as those that make the voices of the native healthy substrata of Mannahatta young
men, especially the drivers of horses and
all whose work leads to free loud calling
and commanding, have such a ring and
freshness.

Pronunciation of Yankees is nasal and
offensive — it has the flat tones. — It could
probably be changed by placing only those
teachers in schools who have rich ripe voices
— and by the children practicing to speak
from the chest and in the guttural and bari-
tone (methods) voice. All sorts of physical,
moral, and mental deformities are inevitably
returned in the voice.

The races that in their realities are sup-
ple, obedient, cringing, have hundreds of

words to express hundreds of forms of acts, thoughts, flanges, of those realities, which the English tongue knows nothing of.

The English tongue is full of strong words native or adopted to express the blood-born passion of the race for rudeness and resistance, as against polish and all acts to give in: robust, brawny, athletic, muscular, acrid, harsh, rugged, severe, pluck, grit, effrontery, stern, resistance, bracing, rude, rugged, rough, shaggy, bearded, arrogant, haughty. These words are alive and sinewy — they walk, look, step with an air of command. — They will often lead the rest — they will not follow. — How can they follow? — They will appear strange in company unlike themselves.

English words. — Even people's names were spelt by themselves, sometimes one way sometimes another. — Public necessity remedies all troubles. — Now, in the 80th year of These States, there is a little diversity in the ways of spelling words, and much diversity in the ways of pronouncing them; — steamships, railroads, newspapers, submarine telegraphs, will probably bring them in. — If not, it is not important.

11

So in the accents and inflections of words. — Language must cohere — it cannot be left loosely to float or to fly away. — Yet all the rules of the accents and inflections of words, drop before a perfect voice — that may follow the rules or be ignorant of them — it is indifferent which. — Pronunciation is the stamina of language, — it is language. — The noblest pronunciation, in a city or race, marks the noblest city or race, or descendants thereof.

Why are names (words) so mighty ? — Because facts, ancestry, maternity, faiths, are. — Slowly, sternly, inevitably, move the souls of the earth, and names (words) are its (their) signs.

Kosmos words, Words of the *Free Expansion of Thought, History, Chronology, Literature*, are showing themselves, with foreheads, muscular necks and breasts. — These gladden me. — I put my arms around them — touch my lips to theirs. The past hundred centuries have confided much to me, yet they mock me, frowning. — I think I am done with many of the words of the past hundred centuries. — I am mad that their poems, bibles, words, still rule and represent the earth, and are not yet superseded. — But why do I say so ? — I must not, will not, be impatient.

In American city excursions, for military practice, for firing at the target, for all the exercises of health and manhood — why should not women accompany them ? — I expect to see the time in Politics, Business, Public Gatherings, Processions, Excitements, when women shall not be divided from men, but shall take their part on the same terms as men. What sort of women have Massachusetts, Ohio, Virginia, Pennsylvania, and the rest, correspondent with what they continually want ? Sometimes I have fancied that only from superior, hardy women can rise the future superiorities of These States.

Man's words, for the young men of these states, are all words that have arisen out of the qualities of mastership, going first, brunting danger first, — words to identify a hardy boyhood — knowledge — an erect, sweet, lusty, body, without taint — choice and chary of its love-power.

The spelling of words is subordinate. — Morbidness for nice spelling, and tenacity for or against some one letter or so, means dandyism and impotence in literature. — Of course the great writers must have digested all these things, — passed lexicons, etymologies, orthographies, through them and extracted the nutriment. — Modern taste is for brevity and for ranging words in spelling classes ; — probably, the words of the English tongue can never be ranged in spelling classes. The Phonetic (?) Spelling is on natural principles — it has arbitrary forms of letters and combinations of letters, for all sounds. — It may in time prevail — it surely will prevail if it is best it should. — For many hundred years there was nothing like settled spelling.

A perfect user of words uses things — they exude in power and beauty from him — miracles from his hands — miracles from his mouth — lilies, clouds, sunshine, woman, poured copiously — things, whirled like chain-shot rocks, defiance, compulsion, houses, iron, locomotives, the oak, the pine, the keen eye, the hairy breast, the Texan ranger, the Boston truckman, the woman that arouses a man, the man that arouses a woman.

Tavern words, such as have reference to drinking, or the compliments of those who drink — the names of some three hundred different American tavern-drinks in one part or another of These States.

Words of all degrees of dislike, from just a tinge, onward or deepward.

Words of approval, admiration, friendship. This is to be said among the young men of These States, that with a wonderful tenacity of friendship, and passionate fondness for their friends, and always a manly readiness to make friends, they yet have remarkably few words of names for the friendly sentiments. — They seem to be words that do not thrive here among the muscular classes, where the real quality of friendship is always freely to be found. — Also, they are words which the muscular classes, the young men of these states, rarely use, and have an aversion for ; — they never give words to their most ardent friendships.

Words of politics are numerous in these states, and many of them peculiar. — The western states have terms of their own : the President's message — the political meeting — the committees — the resolutions : new vegetables — new trees — new animals.

If success and breed follow the camels and dromedaries, that are now just introduced into Texas, to be used for travel and traffic over the vast wilds between the lower Mississippi and the Pacific, a number of new words will also have to be tried after them.

The appetite of the people of These States, in popular speeches and writings, is for un-hemmed latitude, coarseness, directness, live epithets, expletives, words of opprobrium, re-sistance. — This I understand because I have the taste myself as large as largely as any one. — I have pleasure in the use, on fit occa-sions, of traitor, coward, liar, shyster, skulk, doughface, trickster, mean curse, backslider, thief, impotent, lickspittle.

The great writers are often select of their audiences. — The greatest writers only are well-pleased and at their ease among the un-learned — are received by common men and women familiarly, do not hold out obscure, but come welcome to table, bed, leisure, by day and night.

A perfect writer would make words sing, dance, kiss, do the male and female act, bear children, weep, bleed, rage, stab, steal, fire cannon, steer ships, sack cities, charge with cavalry or infantry, or do any thing, that man or woman or the natural powers can do.

Latent, in a great user of words, must ac-tually be all passions, crimes, trades, animals, stars, God, sex, the past, might, space, metals,

16

and the like — because these are the words, and he who is not these, plays with a foreign tongue, turning helplessly to dictionaries and authorities. — How can I tell you ? — I put many things on record that you will not understand at first — perhaps not in a year — but they must be (are to be) understood. — The earth, I see, writes with prodigal clear hands all summer, forever, and all winter also, content, and certain to be understood in time — as, doubtless, only the greatest user of words himself fully enjoys and understands himself.

Words of Names of Places are strong, copious, unruly, in the repertoire for American pens and tongues. The Names of These States — the names of Countries, Cities, Rivers, Mountains, Villages, Neighborhoods — poured plentifully from each of the languages that graft the English language — or named from some natural peculiarity of water or earth, or some event that happened there — often named, from death, from some animal, from some of those subtle analogies that the common people are so quick to perceive. — The names in the list of the Post Offices of These States are studies.

What name a city has — What name a

State, river, sea, mountain, wood, prairie, has
— is no indifferent matter. — All aboriginal
names sound good. I was asking for something savage and luxuriant, and behold here
are the aboriginal names. I see how they are
being preserved. They are honest words —
they give the true length, breadth, depth.
They all fit. Mississippi! — the word winds
with chutes — it rolls a stream three thousand
miles long. Ohio, Connecticut, Ottawa,
Monongahela, all fit.

Names are magic. — One word can pour
such a flood through the soul. — To-day I will
mention Christ's before all other names. —
Grand words of names are still left. — What
is it that flows through me at the sight of the
word Socrates, or Cincinnatus, or Alfred of
the olden time — or at the sight of the word
Columbus, or Shakespeare, or Rousseau, or
Mirabeau — or at the sight of the word Washington, or Jefferson, or Emerson?

Out of Christ are divine words — out of
this savior. Some words are fresh-smelling,
like lilies, roses, to the soul, blooming without
failure. — The name of Christ — all words
that have arisen from the life and death of
Christ, the divine son, who went about speaking perfect words, no patois — whose life was

perfect, — the touch of whose hands and feet was miracles — who was crucified — his flesh laid in a shroud, in the grave.[1]

Words of Names of Persons, thus far, still return the old continents and races — return the past three thousand years — perhaps twenty thousand — return the Hebrew Bible, Greece, Rome, France, the Goths, the Celts, Scandinavia, Germany, England. Still questions come : What flanges are practicable for names of persons that mean These States ? — What is there in the best aboriginal names ? What is there in strong words of qualities, bodily, mental, — a name given to the cleanest and most beautiful body, or to the offspring of the same ? — What is there that will conform to the genius of These States, and to all the facts ? — What escape with perfect freedom, without affectation, from the shoals of Johns, Peters, Davids, Marys ? Or on what happy principle, popular and fluent, could other words be prefixed or suffixed to these,

---

[1] Whitman here inserts a memorandum, a sort of self-query, to this effect : " A few characteristic words — words give us to see — (list of poets — Hindoo — Homer — Shakespeare — Pythagoras, Plato, Zoroaster, Menu, Socrates, Sesostris, Christ). Improve this." — H. T.

to make them show who they are, what land they were born in, what government, which of The States, what genius, mark, blood, times, have coined them with strong-cut coinage?

The subtle charm of the beautiful pronunciation is not in dictionaries, grammars, marks of accent, formulas of a language, or in any laws or rules. The charm of the beautiful pronunciation of all words, of all tongues, is in perfect flexible vocal organs, and in a developed harmonious soul. — All words, spoken from these, have deeper sweeter sounds, new meanings, impossible on any less terms. — Such meanings, such sounds, continually wait in every word that exists — in these words — perhaps slumbering through years, closed from all tympans of temples, lips, brains, until that comes which has the quality patiently waiting in the words. The blank left by words wanted, but unsupplied, has sometimes an unnamably putrid cadaverous meaning. It talks louder than tongues. What a stinging taste is left in that literature and conversation where have not yet been served up by resistless consent, words to be freely used in books, rooms, at table, any where, to specifically mean the act male and female.

Likely there are other words wanted. — Of words wanted, the matter is summed up in this : When the time comes for them to represent any thing or any state of things, the words will surely follow. The lack of any words, I say again, is as historical as the existence of words. As for me, I feel a hundred realities, clearly determined in me, that words are not yet formed to represent. Men like me — also women, our counterparts, perfectly equal — will gradually get to be more and more numerous — perhaps swiftly, in shoals ; then the words will also follow, in shoals. — It is the glory and superb rose-hue of the English language, any where, that it favors growth as the skin does — that it can soon become, wherever that is needed, the tough skin of a superior man or woman.

The art of the use of words would be a stain, a smutch, but for the stamina of things. For in manners, poems, orations, music, friendship, authorship, what is not said is just as important as what is said, and holds just as much meaning. — Fond of men, as a living woman is — fond of women, as a living man is.

I like limber, lasting, fierce words. — I like them applied to myself — and I like them in

newspapers, courts, debates, congress. — Do
you suppose the liberties and the brawn of
These States have to do only with delicate
lady-words ? with gloved gentleman-words ?
Bad Presidents, bad judges, bad clients, bad
editors, owners of slaves, and the long ranks
of Northern political suckers (robbers, traitors,
suborned), monopolists, infidels, castrated
persons, impotent persons, shaved persons,
supplejacks, ecclesiastics, men not fond of
women, women not fond of men, cry down
the use of strong, cutting, beautiful, rude
words. To the manly instincts of the People
they will forever be welcome.

In words of names, the mouth and ear of
the people show antipathy to titles, misters,
handles. They love short first names abbre-
viated to their lips : Tom, Bill, Jack. — These
are to enter into literature, and be voted
for on political tickets for the great offices.
Expletives, words naming the act male and
female, curious words and phrases of assent
or inquiry, nicknames either to persons or
customs. (Many actions, many kinds of
character, and many of the fashions of dress
have names among two thirds of the people,
that would never be understood among the
remaining third, and never appear in print.)

Factories, mills, and all the processes of hundreds of different manufacturers grow thousands of words. Cotton, woollen, and silk goods — hemp, rope, carpets, paper-hangings, paints, roofing preparations, hardware, furniture, paper mills, the printing offices with their wonderful improvements, engraving, daguerreotyping.

This is the age of the metal Iron. *Iron, with all that it does, or that belongs to iron, or flanges from it,* results in words : from the mines they have been drawn, as the ore has been drawn. — Following the universal laws of words, these are welded together in hardy forms and characters. — They are ponderous, strong, definite, not indebted to the antique — they are iron words, wrought and cast. — I see them all good, faithful, massive, permanent words. I love well these iron words of 1856. — *Coal* has its words also, that assimilate very much with those of iron.

Gold of course has always its words. — The mint, the American coinage, the dollar piece, the fifty dollar or one hundred dollar piece — California, the metallic basis of banking, chemical tests of gold — all these have their words : Canada words, Yankee words, Mannahatta words, Virginia words,

Florida and Alabama words, Texas words, Mexican and Nicaraguan words; California words, Ohio, Illinois, and Indiana words.

The different mechanics have different words — all, however, under a few great over-arching laws. — These are carpenter's words, mason's words, blacksmith's words, shoemaker's words, tailor's words, hatter's words, weaver's words, painter's words.

The *Farmer's words* are immense. — They are mostly old, partake of ripeness, home, the ground — have nutriment, like wheat and milk. Farm words are added to, now, by a new class of words, from the introduction of chemistry into farming, and from the introduction of numerous machines into the barn and field.

The nigger dialect furnishes hundreds of outré words, many of them adopted into the common speech of the mass of the people. — Curiously, these words show the old English instinct for wide open pronunciations, as *yallah* for yellow — *massah* for master — and for rounding off all the corners of words. The nigger dialect has hints of the future theory of the modification of all the words of the English language, for musical purposes, for a native grand opera in America, leaving the words just as they are for writing and speaking, but the same words so modified as to answer perfectly for musical purposes, on grand and simple principles. — Then we should have two sets of words, male and female as they should be, in these states, both equally understood by the people, giving a fit much-needed medium to that passion for music, which is deeper and purer in America than in any other land in the world. — The music of America is to adopt the Italian method, and expand it to vaster, simpler, far superber effects. — It is not to be satisfied till it comprehends the people and is comprehended by them.

Sea words, coast words, sloop words, sailor's and boatman's words, words of ships, are numerous in America. — One fourth of the people of these states are aquatic — love the water, love to be near it, smell it, sail on it, swim in it, fish, clam, trade to and fro upon it. To be much on the water, or in constant sight of it, affects words, the voice, the passions. — Around the markets, among the fish-smacks, along the wharves, you hear a thousand words, never yet printed in the repertoire of any lexicon — words, strong words solid as logs, and more beauty to me than any of the antique.

Words of the Laws of the Earth,
Words of the Stars, and about them,
Words of the Sun and Moon,
Words of Geology, History, Geography,
Words of Ancient Races,
Words of the Medieval Races,
Words of the progress of Religion, Law, Art, Government,
Words of the surface of the Earth, grass, rocks, trees, flowers, grains and the like,
Words of like climates,
Words of the Air and Heavens,
Words of the Birds of the air, and of insects,
Words of Animals,
Words of Men and Women — the hundreds of different nations, tribes, colors, and other distinctions,
Words of the Sea,
Words of Modern Leading Ideas,
Words of Modern Inventions, Discoveries, engrossing Themes, Pursuits,
Words of These States—the Year 1, Washington, the Primal Compact, the Second Compact (namely the Constitution)—

trades, farms, wild lands, iron, steam,
slavery, elections, California, and so forth,
Words of the Body, Senses, Limbs, Surface,
Interior,
Words of dishes to eat, or of naturally pro-
duced things to eat,
Words of clothes,
Words of implements,
Words of furniture,
Words of all kinds of Building and Con-
structing,
Words of Human Physiology,
Words of Human Phrenology,
Words of Music,
Words of Feebleness, Nausea, Sickness,
Ennui, Repugnance, and the like.

In most instances a characteristic word
once used in a poem, speech, or what not, is
then exhausted; he who thinks he is going
to produce effects by freely using strong
words, is ignorant of words. One single
name belongs to one single place only —
as a key-word of a book may be best used
only once in the book. — A true composition
in words, returns the human body, male or
female — that is the most perfect composition, and shall be best-beloved by men and

women, and shall last the longest, which slights no part of the body, and repeats no part of the body. — To make a perfect composition in words is more than to make the best building or machine, or the best statue, or picture. — It shall be the glory of the greatest masters to make perfect compositions in words.

As wonderful delineations of character — as the picturesque of men, women, history — these plays of Shakespeare and the rest are grand — our obligations to them are incalculable. Other facts remain to be considered — their foreignness to us in much of their spirit — the sentiment under which they were written, that caste is not to be questioned — that the nobleman is of one blood and the —

Costumes are retrospective — they rise out of the substrata of education, equality, ignorance, caste and the like. A nation that imports its costumes imports deformity. — Shall one man be afraid, or one woman be afraid, to dress in a beautiful, decorous, natural, wholesome, inexpensive manner, because many thousands dress in the reverse manner? There is this, also, about costumes — many save themselves from being exiled, and keep each other in countenance, by being alike foolish, dapper, extravagant. I see that the day is to come very soon in America when there will not be a flat level of costumes.

Probably there is this truth to be said about the Anglo-Saxon breed — that in real vocal use it has less of the words of the various phases of friendship and love than any other race, and more friendship and love. The literature, so full of love, is begotten of the old Celtic metrical romances, and of the extravagant lays of those who sang and narrated, in France, and thence in England — and of Italian extravaganzas — and all that sighing, vowing, kissing, dying, that was in songs in European literature in the sixteenth century. — Still, it seems as if this love-sickness engrafted on our literature were only a fair response and enjoyment that people nourish themselves with, after repressing their words. — The Americans, like the English, probably make love worse than any other race. — Voices follow character, and nothing is better than a superb vocalism. I think this land is covered with the weeds and chaff of literature.

California is sown thick with the names

of all the little and big saints. Chase them away and substitute aboriginal names. What is the fitness — What the strange charm of aboriginal names ? — Monongahela — it rolls with venison richness upon the palate. Among names to be revolutionized : that of the city of " Baltimore."

Never will I allude to the English Language or tongue without exultation. This is the tongue that spurns laws, as the greatest tongue must. It is the most capacious vital tongue of all — full of ease, definiteness and power — full of sustenance. — An enormous treasure-house, or range of treasure houses, arsenals, granary, chock full with so many contributions from the north and from the south, from Scandinavia, from Greece and Rome — from Spaniards, Italians and the French, — that its own sturdy home-dated Angles-bred words have long been outnumbered by the foreigners whom they lead — which is all good enough, and indeed must be. — America owes immeasurable respect and love to the past, and to many ancestries, for many inheritances — but of all that America has received from the past, from the mothers and fathers of laws, arts, letters, &c., by far the greatest inheritance is the

English Language — so long in growing — so fitted.

All the greatness of any land, at any time, lies folded in its names. — Would I recall some particular country or age? the most ancient? the greatest? — I recall a few names — a mountain, or sierra of mountains — a sea or bay — a river — some mighty city — some deed of persons, friends or enemies, — some event, perhaps a great war, perhaps a greater peace — some time-marking and place-marking philosoph, divine person, king, bard, goddess, captain, discoverer, or the like. — Thus does history, in all things, hang around a few names. — Thus does all human interest hang around names. — All men experience it, but no man ciphers it out.

What is the curious rapport of names? — I have been informed that there are people who say it is not important about names — one word is as good as another, if the designation be understood. — I say that nothing is more important than names. — Is art important? Are forms? Great clusters of nomenclature in a land (needed in American nomenclature) include appropriate names for the Months (those now used perpetuate old myths); appropriate names for the Days of

AN AMERICAN PRIMER

the Week (those now used perpetuate Teutonic and Greek divinities); appropriate names for Persons American — men, women, and children; appropriate names for American places, cities, rivers, counties, &c. — The word county itself should be changed. Numbering the streets, as a general thing, with a few irresistible exceptions, is very good. No country can have its own poems without it have its own names. — The name of Niagara should be substituted for the St. Lawrence. Among the places that stand in need of fresh appropriate names are the great cities of St. Louis, New Orleans, St. Paul's.

The whole theory and practice of the naming of College societies must be remade on superior American principles. — The old theory and practice of classical education is to give way, and a new race of teachers is to appear. — I say we have here, now, a greater age to celebrate, greater ideas to embody, than anything ever in Greece or Rome — or in the names of Jupiters, Jehovahs, Apollos and their myths. The great proper names used in America must commemorate things belonging to America and dating thence. — Because, what is America for? — To commemorate the old myths and the gods ? — To repeat the Mediterranean here ? Or the uses and growths of Europe here ? — No ; — (Nä-o-o) but to destroy all those from the purposes of the earth, and to erect a new earth in their place.

All lies folded in names. I have heard it said that when the spirit arises that does not brook submission and imitation, it will throw off the ultramarine names. — That Spirit already walks the streets of the cities of These States — I, and others, illustrate it. — I say America, too, shall be commemorated — shall stand rooted in the ground in names — and shall flow in the water in names and be diffused in time, in days, in months, in their names. — Now the days signify extinct gods and goddesses — the months half-unknown rites and emperors — and chronology with the rest is all foreign to America — all exiles and insults here.

But it is no small thing — no quick growth ; not a matter of rubbing out one word and of writing another. — Real names never come so easily. — The greatest cities, the greatest politics, the greatest physiology and soul, the greatest orators, poets, and literati — The best women, the freest leading men, the proudest national character —

33

such, and the like, are indispensable beforehand. — Then the greatest names will follow, for they are results — and there are no greater results in the world.

Names are the turning point of who shall be master. — There is so much virtue in names that a nation which produces its own names, haughtily adheres to them, and subordinates others to them, leads all the rest of the nations of the earth. — I also promulge that a nation which has not its own names, but begs them of other nations, has no identity, marches not in front but behind.

Names are a test of the esthetic and of spirituality. — A delicate subtle something there is in the right name — an undemonstrable nourishment that exhilarates the soul. Masses of men, unaware what they like, lazily inquire what difference there is between one name and another. — But the few fine ears of the world decide for them also and recognize them — the masses being always as eligible as any whether they know it or not. — All that immense volumes, and more than volumes, can tell, are conveyed in the right name. The right name of a city, state, town, man, or woman, is a perpetual feast to the esthetic and moral nature.

Names of Newspapers. What has such a name as The Ægis, The Mercury, The Herald, to do in America?

Californian, Texan, New Mexican, and Arizonian names have the sense of the ecstatic monk, the cloister, the idea of miracles, and of devotees canonized after death. — They are the results of the early missionaries and the element of piety in the old Spanish character. — They have, in the same connection, a tinge of melancholy and of a curious freedom from roughness and money-making. Such names stand strangely in California. What do such names know of democracy, — of the hunt for the gold leads and the nugget or of the religion that is scorn and negation?

American writers are to show far more freedom in the use of words. — Ten thousand native idiomatic words are growing, or are to-day already grown, out of which vast numbers could be used by American writers, with meaning and effect — words that would be welcomed by the nation, being of the national blood — words that would give that taste of identity and locality which is so dear in literature.

AFTERWORD

TO SAY that Walt Whitman was in love with words is hardly more than saying he was a real poet. All genuine poets are in love with words. They are the medium of their art. Poets not only collect what the epic poet in *Beowulf* called his "word-hoard," but they brood on their meaning, dissect and experiment with their nuances. We might guess this from Whitman's poems, but in the miscellany of notes which Horace Traubel published as *An American Primer* we have the proof of Whitman's infatuation with words.

For individual poems Whitman often made lists of words for possible use. He began this practice as early as the composition of his 1855 poems, and in September 1883 he was still doing it as he sat on the beach at Ocean Grove, N.J. trying to find "Adverbs, adjectives &c" suggested by the sea surf (see *The Solitary Singer*, 513).

Whitman himself did not know what to call the bundle of notes published after his death as *An American Primer*. He told Traubel he had thought of using these notes

37

for a lecture, but apparently never did. They might have made an interesting lecture if he could have provoked in his audience the same enthusiasm he felt in writing them. "Names are magic," he says. Here he refers specifically to proper names, but he felt the same way about the names of objects, actions, qualities, and relations. "One word can pour such a flood through the soul." (18)

An American Primer is no ordinary textbook guide or manual. In Whitman's mind the notes did convey what he thought was most basic in language. But to understand that, we must know something of the Emersonian or "transcendental" theory of language. I call it Emersonian because Whitman probably got it from hearing Emerson's lecture on "The Poet" in New York in 1842, which Whitman reported for the *New York Aurora.* Emerson had more fully expressed this theory in 1836 in *Nature,* but I find no evidence that Whitman read it until later, when Emerson set him to "boiling," to use Whitman's own word.

The theory was that words are symbols of things in nature, but nature itself is only a symbol of a spiritual reality transcending the world of the senses. In "The Poet" (*Essays* version) Emerson says:

Things admit of being used as symbols, because nature is a symbol, in the whole, and in every part. Every line we can draw in the sand, has expression; and there is no body without its spirit or genius. All form is an effect of character; all condition, of the quality of life; all harmony, of health; (and, for this reason, a perception of beauty should be sympathetic, or proper only to the good).

Whitman believed that words acquired their meaning not from dictionaries but from the people who used them, from the character, the intentions, and the experiences of the users of the words. Now, without regard to transcendental theory, this is also sound *semantic* doctrine. I. A. Richards and William Empson taught us that words are far more ambiguous and complex in meaning than most people had ever imagined. *Meanings* are subtle, and vary with each user. And a corrupt user corrupts the words he uses. Whitman knew that when he wrote "The Eighteenth Presidency!" One political party flaunted "Americanism" without "feeling the first aspirstion of it";

39

while the other had so degraded the word "democracy" that "What the so-called democracy are now sworn to perform would eat the faces off the succeeding generations of common people worse than the most horrible disease."

The burden of Whitman's message in his 1855 Preface is that a perfect user of words (which the ideal poet should be) must himself be a perfect person. Repeatedly in *An American Primer* he exhorts his reader to cultivate the kind of life which will give positive meaning to the words he uses. In 1856 in "Poem of the Sayers of the Words of the Earth" (later called "Song of the Rolling Earth") he asks:

> Were you thinking that those were the
>   words – those upright lines? those
>   curves, angles, dots?
> No, those are not the words – the
>   substantial words are in the ground and
>   sea,
> They are in the air – they are in you.

Thus Whitman's philosophical theory also has its ethical, esthetic, and practical aspect.

Whitman was also surprisingly right in his linguistic assumptions. All languages have evolved from a verbal stage; speech preceded writing by thousands of years, maybe even millions. And the spoken language is still more flexible and capable of growth. Whitman was right, too, in believing that English was one of the most tolerant languages to change, always enriching itself by borrowing freely from other languages. The French people founded an academy to stabilize their language, but the English people would not tolerate an academy, and the attempt of a few Federalists in the early years of the American Republic to start an academy got nowhere.

Whitman expected the spread of the English language mainly because he anticipated an enormous increase in American speakers of it. He did not foresee that English would become a world language in the twentieth century. This has come about partly because of the political power, first, of the British Empire, and then of the United States and the British Commonwealth. But the nature of the English language has aided its spread. Whitman also welcomed American variations on British

English, but he was not so chauvinistic as to advocate a separate "American language." No one was more patriotic than he, but he knew that American speech was basically English, like Canadian English, Australian English, or New Zealand English.

Whitman thought that possibly *Leaves of Grass* might be only "a language experiment," and that it was in many ways. But it was a radical experiment like James Joyce's, or even Wordsworth's – in theory, not actual practice. Many scholars have studied the influence of the spoken lanuage on Whitman's rhythms and prosodic patterns, and undoubtedly the influence was enormous. But his vocabulary was as "literary" as it was colloquial. He called slang a living language, and he sometimes used current slang words, but not enough to characterize his style – or to debase it. And for all his denunciations of prudery, he did not use the tabooed four-letter words. Yet perhaps he did resent the fact that they were tabooed, for he bitterly denounced censorship in *An American Primer* (20):

The blank left by words wanted, but unsupplied, has sometimes an unnamably putrid cadaverous

meaning. It talks louder than tongues. What a
stinging taste is left in that literature and conversation where have not yet been served up by
resistless consent, words to be freely used in
books, rooms, at table, anywhere, to specifically
mean the act male and female.

Whitman got around this taboo by the most
imaginative and expressive use of symbolical imagery and kinetic rhythms to convey
vicariously sex acts. One example is the
symbolical insemination in "Song of Myself," sec. 29. Another is the "bride-groom
night of love" in "I Sing the Body Electric,"
sec. 5. Though I also disapprove of censorship, I am not sure that Whitman's literary
subterfuge was not an artistic bonus, for to
me these passages are unsurpassed in sen-
suous poetry.

But to return to the theme of *An American Primer,* these are also examples of
Whitman's having poured new meanings
into the contexts of his lyricism. Often in
Leaves of Grass he succeeds in giving words
the life and beauty he advocated. The
American Primer will continue to reward
the reader with each reading. And this, I
think, is because it is really a prose poem,

43

which draws perennial life from Whitman's
infatuation with words.

−Gay Wilson Allen, author of
*The Solitary Singer: A Critical
Biography of Walt Whitman*

This new printing of *An American Primer* is reproduced from the original edition published by Small, Maynard & Company in 1904. See William White, ed., *Daybooks and Notebooks* (New York: New York University Press, 1978), 3:728–757 for a complete presentation of Walt Whitman's text for *An American Primer*. I'd like to acknowledge the advice and encouragement of Ed Folsom, William White, C. Carroll Hollis, and Gay Wilson Allen as well as financial support provided by Charles E. Feinberg and the National Endowment for the Arts in Washington, D.C.

—Jim Perlman, co-editor of
*Walt Whitman: The Measure
of His Song*

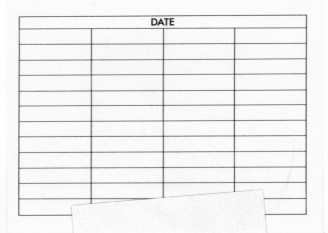

DATE			

R0158495411   HUM   814 W615

HOUSTON PUBLIC LIBRARY

CENTRAL LIBRARY
500 MCKINNEY

© THE BAKER & TAYLOR CO.